1

Introduction

My goal is to give you the very best advice on how you can become brilliant at writing essays. Having researched many books and articles, I realized there is a noticeable absence of well written and accessible guides to writing essays. In order to remedy this, I brought together the best information in the field and condensed it down.

Unlike many books, there are no sections of "filler" information. I have edited and cut down ruthlessly to bring to you a book which, I hope, will give the clearest guidance. I also wanted to pack this book with practical and easily actionable ideas. I don't want you to walk away from this book with a glut of information that isn't directly helpful to your essay writing, so much of it you will be able to put to use right away!

This book is roughly divided into two sections. First, I will cover a step-by-step process to writing a great essay. Second, I will go through a series of principles and techniques that will allow you to create an essay at high speed. Fusing the advice from each section will provide you with a complete tool set to write a great essay in 8 hours or less. However, please bear in mind that the promise of an 8-hour essay is only possible for more modest essay lengths. For essays longer than 3,000 words, it is in my experience, difficult to write something of quality within 8 hours.

Now, let's begin your crash course on essay writing!

The Great Essay: Choosing the Right Question

This advice is only applicable if you are given the option of choosing your essay topic/title. If this is not relevant for you, feel free to skip to the next chapter.

When choosing your essay title, it is important to achieve a suitably narrow focus. You do not want a title that is too expansive because it will then be harder to cover every important point that needs to be addressed. The other side of this is also true: you do not want to create a title that is so tight in its focus that you can't find enough sources, and so don't have enough of value to say on the subject.

There is nothing worse than sinking hours into an essay, only to realize that there is not enough material to create a piece of interesting work. Students normally go the other way and pick a very expansive title because they think that this will be easier to write, and in a manner it is. It is certainly a little safer to opt for a title that describes a broader topic, but be careful; your task can become daunting as you attempt to summarize large amounts of information, and are unable to find the time to closely analyze a given source.

Attempt to find a balance so that you do not run out of things to say, but also don't waste time covering huge amounts of ground at the expense of achieving a precise, focused analysis. Do a small amount of research before you choose a title in order to estimate how much material you can create for your essay title before you commit.

The Great Essay: Begin with a Question

Questions are the best way to begin an essay, as effective writing needs to address a question. An essay is then all about finding a resolution: an answer that becomes your thesis. Developing an essay around a question also helps our writing to be more specific and helps you stick to a definite course.

If you can choose your essay title, it is often a good idea to make it a question. If you have been given a title that is not a question (or feel it best to have a title that is not a question), always rearrange the title briefly to help your understanding and make working with the essay easier.

The answer to the question is the core of your essay: it is the 'thesis' of your piece. To write a high-quality essay, the thesis must be very clear and definite. A strong piece of writing comes from a confident and unambiguous answer to a question. Without this your writing will be weak and ineffective, and will not get you a good grade. These aspects build on each other like the foundations of a house: without a clear and narrow focus, a good question, and a strong thesis, your essay will be less likely to succeed.

When defining your thesis, it is also a good idea to use superlatives to make it as strong as possible. This is especially true for a piece of journalism or for commercial writing. Using superlatives will grab the attention of the reader and suck them into purchasing what you are selling. When studying, it depends on the establishment and what purpose you are writing for; inquire as to what is encouraged. A great essay title could be: "The Most Important Reason the North Won the Civil War." Notice that this is more interesting and compelling than the more lackluster "Why the North Won the Civil War."

The Great Essay: Researching

Researching your essay well is extremely important. It is essential you do not miss any of the important aspects that must be included in the essay. Therefore, it is best to initially cast a net to find what must be included. You may later do more specific research with a "hook and line" to discover the details that will create a complete picture.

For the preliminary "net casting," it can be a good idea to find a short and succinct source; a source that provides a summary of everything you will be writing on. If your essay itself is relatively short, say less than 3,000 words, perhaps use three good sources that provide overviews of the topic. Find where these sources overlap and you will begin to understand the more important aspects to be included. This is not a precise art, but over time you will develop a feel for how much research needs to be done. But try to use at least three sources for the initial overview. Additionally, if a source seems more reputable and better written, focus more on that one.

These initial sources, which give a good overview of the topic, will act as a guide to your further research. Depending on how niche / how popular your essay title is, you will have to vary the time you spend researching. If it is a unique title that has not had much written on it before, you will have to spend a lot of time researching. However, more often than not this will only be necessary in the final stages of a university course. Up to this point you will be able to find quality information fairly easily.

The Internet is the easiest place to start researching, especially if you are struggling to begin to work on your essay. Quickly Googling the main aspects of your essay should reveal enough information to push you in the right direction. For the detailed research that comes later, use online databases of articles and, of course, the best library available.

The Great Essay: Planning

The plan is all about getting your best ideas down on paper so you know what you are going to address in the essay. Start building the plan once you have a good amount of research material assembled. When beginning to plan, don't feel that you must have a perfect collection of research and have read everything. Just have enough sources at hand to feel fairly confident that you could finish an OK essay with those alone. Once the plan is developed, you can flesh out the research as needed.

The plan you build is not a perfect model for the essay, so be flexible and ready to change things. The essay itself may turn out quite differently from the plan you make at first. Do not get attached to the plan you make, as it is nothing more than a possible course, a guide that helps you find the next step. If needed, return to the plan throughout your essay writing and amend, adapt, and improve it as you see fit, and as new ideas come to light.

A quick note on planning for essay-based exams:

For exam essays, making a plan is typically a good idea, but make sure it is a quick plan. There is nothing worse than wasting precious exam time by trying to create a perfect plan or to procrastinate on actually writing the essay by making a plan.

Spend, at most, five minutes on this. Two minutes will probably be ideal.

The only thing you need to do is jot down the most important 3-6 points you want to cover and perhaps a note of quotations you can draw on to support them. A plan for an essay exam is normally a good idea, but you don't have to make one. If you are well prepared and have completed many practice essays, you may not need to. In which case you can leap into the essay writing and begin your introduction.

The Great Essay: Writing an Introduction

An essay must always begin with an introduction. The introduction is a paragraph in which you state, in the clearest manner possible, what your essay will endeavor to do (notice my introduction to this book). Openly state your thesis, keep it simple, and ensure your essay stays on point. The first sentence can be the thesis boiled down to its simplest form, e.g., "The most important reason the North won the Civil War is..."

The introduction needs to only be a short section of the essay. If it is a 3,000 word essay, a 300-400 word introduction would be a good target to aim for. If it is any less, you won't have enough words to clearly present your thesis. There are no hard and fast rules, but I would warn against going much higher than this. Anything over 500 words for a 3,000 word essay will become a waste of time and take up valuable words. Words better spent providing evidence to prove your thesis.

Writing the introduction is normally the first thing you will write, but it can be a better approach to leave writing the introduction until the end when you are writing the conclusion too. This is because occasionally you will have little idea how to answer an essay title. Perhaps you don't know which side of an argument you will support. In this case it can be best (and quicker) to simply begin researching and writing the essay. After you've begun this process, you will be better equipped to discover the side of the argument you find most compelling. You can then return at the end of the essay to write the introduction.

Make the introduction an interesting and poignant entry to your essay that contains the thesis. The introduction draws the reader in and makes them want to read more. If you write a good introduction, the whole essay becomes easier to write. It is the seed that can bloom into a whole essay. A strong introduction will inform the reader what to expect from the essay, helping to make the whole piece clearer, easier to read, and more compelling.

The Great Essay: Grab the Reader's Attention
The first line(s) of your essay and introduction can be important in keeping the reader interested. This advice is more valuable if you are writing an article for a publication or a blog article, and less so for an academic essay. If you are unsure what is appropriate, check with a teacher. Here are two possible ways to grab the reader's attention.

A quotation can be an excellent way to start an essay. A quotation that clearly presents your thesis, or perhaps a quotation that is famously associated with the topic you are writing on is an interesting and exciting way to kick things off. The more articulate and powerfully phrased the quotation, the more you will draw in the reader/marker.

A joke or a story can also be an interesting way to begin a piece of writing. This is especially true if you are writing for entertainment or in a more casual form.

These are just potential ideas; don't feel obliged to start your introduction with them. A "normal" sentence is absolutely fine. "There are many reasons why the North was victorious in the American Civil War…" This is good too.

The Great Essay: Writing the Body

Between the introduction and conclusion there is what I will refer to as the "body" of your essay. This is the core of your piece and is distinctly different from both the introduction and conclusion in regards to its purpose.

When writing the body of your essay, you are attempting to elaborate and describe your thesis whilst consistently providing evidence for why it is true. Depending on the nature of the question and how many words are required, the number of points can vary. A good rule of thumb is to have three main points to support the thesis. Each of these can have smaller sub-points, maybe again three for each. Every one of these contributes like bricks in a wall, and creates the overall presentation and argument for your thesis.

It is a good idea to start with your weakest supporting points and then move to the stronger reasons later. Your essay should always endeavor to be persuasive, making as strong a case as possible for your thesis. Moving from weaker to stronger arguments will create momentum for your argument, and when the conclusion finally comes, the reader will be primed to hear your closing arguments and most inclined to agree with them.

Throughout the essay, in the attempt to elaborate on and prove your thesis, it is essential to provide information from your research as proof. This is a careful blend of revealing your own ideas mixed in with the ideas of others.

The Great Essay: Keep on Topic

Throughout the essay, you need to always be drawing your writing back to the thesis and the central question your essay is endeavoring to answer. If you are not directly answering the question and giving evidence for your answer, you are wasting time. It is as simple as that. Depending on your current experience and skill level at writing essays, this may be an aspect to your work that can boost your grade powerfully.

This simple habit is often the key difference between people who can write good essays and those who can't. Many students think they will get marks for writing down any information related to the topic/essay question. They think they will accrue points for knowledge and understanding, but this is not the case. If your writing does not answer and directly relate back to the title, it is a waste of time.

Even university and college students can be guilty of this. They can raise a crucially important point, but then fail to draw it into the essay and comment on why and how it is relevant to their thesis. Do not be guilty of this; be sure to ALWAYS remain on topic.

Staying on topic contributes to the form of the piece as well. A paragraph should make a point at the start and then give the reasons why it is true. The last sentence of the paragraph summarizes the paragraph's point and puts it into the context of the whole essay.

When learning to keep on topic, it can be useful to make it very obvious that you are staying on point, for example, you can say: "another reason the North won the Civil War is…" Doing this is like writing with training wheels. Later when you have learned to write with more deft complexity, there is no need to use such simple sentence props. But as a beginner, in order to make sure you are always keeping on topic, writing in this manner can be brilliantly helpful.

The Great Essay: Write with Clarity
It is always important to write with lucidity and clarity. A great essay is easy to read and presents ideas in a coherent manner.

The goal is effective communication, and writing with clarity is an essential element to this.

Always err on the side of simple and more easily understood language. Your sentence structure and presentation of ideas needs to be easily consumed by the reader. Until you develop your experience and abilities beyond the humble advice of this book, make writing with clarity a constant priority.

The Great Essay: Present a Balanced Argument (until the end)

Your essay is the presentation of your thesis and what you believe to be true, but it is important to also present the counterarguments to your thesis. An essay needs to be discursive; for every argument you make, present alternative arguments and then comment on which you find compelling and why. Rinse and repeat until the final section of your essay, just before the conclusion, then come down as strongly as possible on the side of the argument you believe to be true, and present your most compelling reasons for this.

Again, there is always room for flexibility; perhaps you go between arguments for your thesis in one paragraph, and then in the following paragraph argue why your thesis is stronger. Writing like this is a straightforward way to create good discourse.

Remember, balance is key to your piece, especially for an academic essay. For articles in journalism balance is less important. Here instead, attention-grabbing ideas and propositions are paramount.

The Great Essay: Using Quotations

Quotations are essential to a good essay. They are the evidence that support the ideas you are presenting. They are like soldiers going into battle to fight for their side of an argument. Look to find powerful and compelling quotations to support your thesis and to give due weighting to counterarguments.

The quotation always requires three aspects, normally in three distinct sentences. These three phases are:

Point

Quotation

Comment

The first phase establishes the context for the quotation and explains and emphasizes why you are using it, for example: "The following quotation demonstrates that industrial strength was a contributing factor to the North winning the Civil War."

The second phase is the quotation itself.

The third phase is your own comment on the quotation. Here you explain how the quotation supports your initial point.

Use quotations regularly; every paragraph of the 'body' of the essay should be littered with quotations. However, take care not to make quotations longer than your own writing. Attempt to work them into your own writing, never letting them dominate the word quota more than necessary. Certainly no more than a quarter of your essay should be made up of quotations.

Additionally, find out how important quotations are in the essay-marking scheme. Sometimes they are essential, and you will be marked on having a certain number of them in your essay. Other times mark schemes view them as more like the icing on the cake.

If you are working to memorize quotations to use in an essay-based exam, be savvy by choosing those that can be used to make a variety of points. For example, pick a quotation that reveals a few themes, as well as the use of language, and so on. This way you can dramatically cut down the number of quotations you need to learn, whilst always having quotations to use in the exam.

The Great Essay: Writing the Conclusion

The final section of the essay is the conclusion. This follows the closing arguments in the body of the essay and brings the entire essay together. The conclusion re-states your thesis alongside the most compelling evidence you have assembled in the body.

If you are unsure about writing your conclusion, go back to the introduction and see what you wrote there. The introduction and conclusion are similar in what they are attempting to do. Both of them talk about the essay as a whole and emphasize the goals of the essay. If you have already written the introduction, look to it for guidance and build upon those ideas to create a more detailed explanation of why your thesis is true. Work to tie the thesis in with the points and evidence you gave throughout the essay. Also mention in brief the counterarguments, along with why they didn't hold sway over the arguments in favor of your thesis.

Do not feel pressured to write the conclusion only at the end of your essay, nor to write your introduction first. If you have a very clear thesis and know exactly where your essay is going, it is easiest to write the introduction first and the conclusion last. Often, however, you will not be able to enjoy such clarity with your essay. In this case, it may be easiest to write your introduction last and perhaps compose your conclusion half way through, when you finally feel clarity as to where the essay must end. There are no definite rules, and often you will have to adapt your approach depending on how well you are engaging with the essay.

The Great Essay: Editing
It takes returning to an essay and reworking the ideas again and again to fashion something great. Editing will be half the battle, so always set aside time and expect to invest in reading over your essay and improving it repeatedly.

Editing improves the text, making it more effective in every way. Work on things like clarity, grammar, and creating balanced arguments. All of these things will need to be worked on and honed again and again to achieve a great essay.

Many students resist editing their essay because they believe it is not worth the time or because they are nervous about the quality of the first draft and perhaps feel embarrassed about reading it again. You must overcome this. Always re-read and edit the essay a minimum of two times.

The extent to which you need to edit your essay will vary based on the quality of the first draft. Obviously, the better research and preparation you do, the better this draft will be, but often even when these are both done excellently, there will still need to be an extensive re-working of the essay. Sometimes just to complete the first draft, you will have to skip between ideas in an odd manner and create a mess of sentences, which will inevitably take a lot of time to re-write and arrange coherently. The time you spend editing will vary for different essays, so expect the worst and set time aside to edit. This process will usually take at least as long as writing the first draft.

It can be a good idea to leave time between edits. "Sleeping on it" can be helpful, or at the very least, take a walk to clear your head. Unless you are writing against the clock, taking time away from the essay will enable you to take a more critical look at it when you return. Leaving time between edits will also help you to come to a deeper understanding of the essay topic. It may be that when you return, your conscious and subconscious minds have found new insights.

The easiest way to edit is in different phases, as doing it all at once in an effort to create a perfect essay can be too much (I will talk more about this in "The 8 Hour Essay"). These "sweeps" will become easier and quicker each time. At first, you will be re-organizing sentences and making the piece more logical. By the final sweep, you will be making small grammatical changes.

Additionally, ensure that you are well aware of the form requirements in your course and follow them precisely: cite quotations, make a complete bibliography, etc. Neglecting this area is the easiest way to lose marks. Formatting accurately only require a small amount of time, so there really is no excuse.

The Great Essay: Proof Read
Once you have edited your essay and are happy with it, do one final sweep to catch all the possible typos that may have crept into the text.

Changing the form you are reading in, for example, by printing the essay out and marking it on paper rather than proofreading on your computer is a great way to help catch typos, as it forces your eyes and mind to interact with the text in a slightly different way. If this seems too much effort (or you don't have the time), a quick trick is to change the font type and/or size. This will help you catch errors by altering the aesthetic of the words on the screen.

It is also a good idea to pass on the work to a friend or colleague – preferably someone with experience with writing and a good eye – as they should be able to catch errors you have missed.

The following section of the book will address how to create an essay at speed: "The 8 Hour Essay."

The 8 Hour Essay: Create a Process

In order to make writing your essay as effective and easy as possible, it is a fantastic idea to create your own process to go through every time you write an essay. In this book I am providing a host of techniques that you can incorporate into your essay-writing process. However, make the final process your own and consider looking to other essay-writing resources, as this book doesn't contain every idea out there.

Perhaps give yourself an hour to research online, then an hour at the local library for your research time, and so on. In finding a process you can repeat, you will ease the pressure on yourself and find it easier each time.

Take the time now to use the tips given earlier in this book to make a step-by-step process for every element of the essay you are writing. Make it simple and effective. Later, I will show you a recommended example process for essay writing.

The 8 Hour Essay: Re-Phrasing

If you can become proficient at quickly rephrasing ideas into your own words, you can become excellent at writing great essays, fast. Ultimately, this is the central aspect to modern academic writing – to research ideas, understand them, and then write them up.

Now, I am definitely not talking about plagiarism. You do not want to plagiarize, ever. Increasingly, faculties and teachers have access to software that uncovers this. But more importantly, you shouldn't plagiarize because – and I know it sounds cliché – you really are cheating yourself, and worst of all, buying into an immature worldview that it is possible to get something for nothing.

To improve your rephrasing skills, practice is very important. Practice writing an essay, but attempt to minimize research and writing time by reading a paragraph or two and then re-writing it into your own words immediately. The better you can get at doing this, the better you will become at writing great essays quickly.

The 8 Hour Essay: Rapid Research

An essential element to researching effectively and quickly is to become better at qualifying potential sources. This means you can rapidly establish whether a source will help you to write your essay or not.

Students often waste a lot of time reading material that is close to the topic of their essay title, but not so close that they would actually use the source. This should be actively avoided. Reading around the topic is absolutely fine if you have a lot of time or want to enjoy the material more. But if you are attempting to write an essay quickly, it is of paramount importance to study only sources that will help you directly answer your essay.

Whenever you are confronted with a possible resource, ask yourself this question: "Is this going to help me write my essay?" Too often students act as if they are instead answering the question, "Is this vaguely related to my essay?" and then begin to read anything and everything they come across.

To quickly ascertain whether a source will be of help to you, it is a great idea to look at the contents page, checking if any of the chapter titles contain relevant key words or phrases. Skimming the introduction, the conclusion, and scanning a few of the pages will also help you to qualify the book more effectively.

Always ensure that the source you are using will directly help you write your essay; wasting time reading things that are related, but won't help you directly, is one of the biggest barriers to writing a great essay quickly.

The 8 Hour Essay: Using Technology Effectively

When writing your essay, there will be many occasions in which the effective use of a computer will greatly increase your ability to create an essay both of quality and at great speed.

*The following techniques are written as if you are working on Microsoft software, but the same approaches are invariably applicable to Apple and other OS' as well.

The most obvious thing to say is that you should be writing on a computer/laptop. If you are writing on paper, even if only for the first draft, you will be sacrificing the various advantages there are to be had by using a computer. Indeed, at every point it is advisable for you to use a computer instead of pen and paper, as the benefits outweigh any drawbacks.

When you compose an essay on a computer, it is much easier to save and retrieve work, edit, and to type new material. In addition, using a keyboard is always quicker than writing with pen and paper. It may, of course, take you a certain amount of time to become competent and speedy with a keyboard, but in time (and with diligent practice) you will certainly be able to write at a prompt pace.

There are many touch-typing lessons available on the Internet. Go to YouTube or similar sites and you will be able to easily find short, quality lessons that will allow you to greatly increase your typing speed.

Buy and use a quality keyboard. If you are using a laptop, consider how the keyboard may not be as comfortable and easy to use as a standalone keyboard. It can also be worth your while to experiment with ergonomic keyboards. There are various designs, so perhaps go to a local tech store and ask to try out a few. If you are writing essays as part of a course, you are going to spend a lot of time with your keyboard, so invest in a quality one that allows you to write quickly and comfortably.

Using a large monitor, or perhaps investing in using two next to each other, will also help you to produce your essay more quickly. The space to have two separate "windows" open at the same time will make taking notes when you are researching online much easier, as you can type straight away from the text you are researching instead of having to minimize and maximize windows again and again.

The space to have two windows open is also handy when editing, as you can have two documents open at the same time. On one side you can put material that needs to be placed within the essay, and the other can be the final essay as it takes shape. Being able to see and work with both simultaneously allows you to easily rearrange your essay without losing material and getting lost in what can become a repetitive copy and pasting process.

When researching online, you will come across many articles and web pages that may seem daunting – sources in which you know there is quality material, but you are reluctant to begin working with the information as it is. There are a couple of tricks to make researching these articles a little easier.

First of all, if you are looking at a long web page or article, you can make it much more manageable to work with if you copy and paste it into a Word document. Once you have done this, you can increase the font size, perhaps convert the font to something more readable, and also get rid of the margins so that text takes up most of the screen, allowing you to scroll down less often. Doing this will make the material easier to read, and will save your eyes, as well as your time, if you have a long article you want to read or scan.

It is also useful to utilize the search function in order to pick out the areas of the text you need to address. The shortcut to do this on a webpage or in Word is "ctrl f." Become familiar with using this as it will save you a great deal of time. Using this function you can skip through what can often be needlessly drawn out articles and immediately find the snippets of information you need. This is another reason why working and researching with technology is more effective, as this function alone can save many hours compared to finding things in a book.

Other shortcuts you can utilize are "ctrl c" to copy, "ctrl x" to cut, and "ctrl v" to paste work. These can save time and energy, particularly when editing or rearranging your essay.

Finally, if the text is too small on a webpage you can use "ctrl +" to zoom in and "ctrl –" to zoom out. This is handy if the article you are reading is presented in an unhelpfully small manner and if, for whatever reason, you don't want to transfer it to a Word document.

Become competent at using tricks like these when writing your essay and you will begin to see the full benefits of using technology to write essays at a much higher speed.

The 8 Hour Essay: Do Not Backtrack When Writing

One of the most powerful ways to increase the speed at which you work is to always focus on doing one phase of the essay at a time. When you are writing your first draft, you are doing that and not attempting to do the final edit and create a perfect final essay.

One of the most common time-wasters when writing an essay is to continually review the work, editing and improving what you have just written. Producing your essay will be much quicker and more effective if you simply keep writing, and only write, when doing your first draft. Do not even re-read what you have written, let alone attempt to improve it.

This will be difficult for some, and it does take a degree of faith in what you are writing, but it is by far a more effective way to write. When you are writing, keep writing, and do not return to what you have done. Later, when it is time to edit, think of it as doing "sweeps" of editing. The initial work you do on the first sweep does not have to produce the perfect, finished article, as you will return to improve it again.

It will become frustrating if you spend too long at a certain point attempting to perfect a given paragraph. It will take up a disproportionate amount of time to bring it to a good standard because you do not let your mind have space to return to it later. Instead, keep the editing process progressive and know that you can return to do another editing sweep once this one is complete. It will otherwise become frustrating and you will lose momentum.

Whatever phase of the essay you are at, focus on that process alone – never back track when writing the first draft, and never attempt to edit something to perfection on the first pass.

The 8 Hour Essay: Write the Easiest Section First

When you are beginning to write your essay, the best place to start is the place you feel most comfortable. Begin writing on whatever aspect of the piece you most enjoy or feel that you could easily write about. There are a few reasons that writing in this way is powerful and will ensure you write better material with increased speed.

If you begin and continue to write on the topics you are most confident about, the essay writing will be easier. The easier it is for you, the faster you will be able to write. When you are working against the clock, there is no time to wait for inspiration or to figure out all the answers.

When you write from what is easiest, you build a powerful momentum in the writing process and you will notice yourself quickly going past word count milestones. This will increase your motivation and sense of achievement as you go, and encourage you to continue writing.

The sheer act of writing consistently from where you feel most comfortable will also mean that you are more likely to enter the state of "flow". In this state, ideas come more easily to you and the working process as a whole feels effortless and enjoyable. When you write in this mode, you will become inspired where next to write as your mind begins to move in a consistent and powerful manner, like water flowing in a river.

The more you can write, the more you will develop understanding of the topic you are writing on. From this understanding, you will be able to further discover where the essay should go next. As you begin to write on one topic and work this out in detail, you will soon be able to address other topics more easily. This is because as you write, your thoughts and ideas will form and re-form organically, revealing insights and connections, which in turn will dynamically reveal possible next steps.

It is not just at the start that you should write from wherever feels easiest/most enjoyable; throughout the essay you should continue this practice, always taking the next step that feels like the most natural progression for your work. Of course, some elements are going to be trickier and you will not want to work on them, but by then you will have developed enough momentum to persevere through.

Writing in this way will make the essay process easier, more effective, and also (perhaps worryingly) enjoyable, as you work in tune with how your mind wants to engage with your essay title.

The 8 Hour Essay: Break Your Essay into Manageable Pieces

The easier you can make the essay writing process, the faster you will do it. A great tip to make essay writing easier is to break the essay into separate elements. The more you can break apart the essay, the more you will be able to work with it in a manageable, effective manner, and in turn complete the essay in less time.

The best way to break your essay into different parts is to do it at the planning stage. Part of the plan should resemble a contents page for the essay you are going to write. Each aspect of the essay needs to be laid out sequentially so that you can work through it step by step. You will need to adapt this plan as you work through the essay; feel free to modify it as you go, but always keep it to hand to make sure that you know (at least vaguely) what there is left to do.

This "contents page" plan will ideally break down your essay into chapters. Each chapter is effectively a paragraph. If these paragraphs are about a half a page, and you adhere at least roughly to the three-point essay structure I discussed earlier in this book, the plan for your essay might look something like this:

Introduction

Point 1: Reason A

Point 1: Reason B

Point 1: Reason C

Point 2: Reason A

Point 2: Reason B

Point 2: Reason C

Point 3: Reason A

Point 3: Reason B

Point 3: Reason C

Conclusion

With this essay structure, you would give three reasons for each point you make. For a standard argumentative essay of perhaps 3,000 words, this basic form can work very well.

Now, when planning your essay – or adapting it as you go – you need simply to write each point and reason alongside these bullet points. This can be a few words or a sentence. Breaking down your essay in this way will enable you to clearly see all the steps that the essay needs to take.

As you write your essay, it will help to make clear divisions between points by writing titles in a bold, different typeface. Be sure you still draw each of these points into the essay as a whole and always cement the main drive for your thesis. Of course, remove these titles when you come to the final editing and completing of your essay. Working with clear divisions and writing titles for paragraphs, works to create definite divisions between parts of your essay and helps you structure and work with your essay more effectively.

Breaking your essay into pieces like this will make the whole thing much less intimidating to work on. You can tackle the research, writing, and editing incrementally – one piece at a time, removing the fear of having too much to do. This fear is one of the reasons so many students leave essay writing to the last minute. The thought of writing 3,000 words and incorporating so many elements (which, at present, are a complete unknown) creates anxiety, which leads to procrastination. Breaking up your essay in this way will make it easier to begin and continue working.

Having manageable chunks of your essay will also make writing the essay easier because you are allowing your mind to focus cleanly on certain elements without it getting distracted and bogged down in others. When you are working on just one element of the essay, you restrict where your mind can go and allow it to work with precision.

Work to divide your essay into manageable pieces and you will make the whole essay writing process quicker and easier. It will allow better planning and organization, encourage your mind to stay cleanly focused on the topic at hand, and also prevent you from becoming perturbed by starting or carrying on with the essay.

The 8 Hour Essay: The 80/20 Pareto Principle

A useful theory to apply to writing essays is the Pareto Principle, which basically states that we can get 80 percent of the results for completing 20 percent of the actions. I would definitely encourage you to Google the Pareto Principle; it is such an important concept that really warrants additional research.

Applying this principle to essay writing will enable you to cut out all the unnecessary time and allow you to write a great essay within 8 hours (and quicker still with practice). When applying this to our essay writing, we attempt to find the most important 20 percent of actions, which will create 80 percent of the essay marks.

The 20 percent of tasks that matter are:

Finding excellent, quality resources. Be ruthless in selection and use only the most important ones. Attempt to cut down research sources to the most valuable few, as this will save time by avoiding reading excessive amounts, the same material, and from needing to switch between sources.

Planning the essay. This is essential, but again, moving away from excessive planning and forethought will allow for a much quicker essay to be written. As I described earlier in this book, a brief plan is very helpful. Plans are always tentative, however, let them move and adjust with time. Trying to stick rigidly to a plan and holding on to a thesis that isn't working will waste a good deal of time and create a poor essay.

Writing the piece. This sounds obvious, but there can often be a good deal of time wasted looking out the window or re-reading words already written when you could be writing more. Becoming brutally honest about when you are writing and when you are not will help to cut down on wasted time. Using time boxing (which will be explained in the following book) is a fantastic way to ensure we apply ourselves to the 20 percent of actual writing and remove the 80 percent on the wasted tasks between these moments.

Look at the other areas of your essay writing and always cut it down to the simplest and most effective actions, which earn 80 percent of results. If you continually work to improve your efforts in these areas, while diminishing the time-wasting habits, you will place yourself firmly on the track to writing a great essay within 8 hours.

The 8 Hour Essay: Bringing it All Together

Let's now take the time to build a workable process for writing a 2,000 word essay.

Think of this as a recipe for managing your efforts and ensuring you write a great essay as quickly as possible.

1 hour spent deciding on the title and speed reading some websites that provide an overview of the topic. Spend 5 minutes of this hour creating a plan.

4 hours spent writing at a rate of at least 500 words per hour. Move between detailed resources found in online journal articles and websites.

2 hours spent editing and improving the text. Do two passes, the first for 90 minutes and the next for 30 minutes.

1 hour building the bibliography, fine-tuning the conclusion, and proofreading.

(For each hour, work for 50 minutes and use the last ten minutes for a break. After four of these work 'hours', take an hour long break for a meal.)

I encourage you to read both of these books twice to solidify the ideas which elaborate on the power of the above process, and then try to write an essay while sticking ruthlessly to the plan above. If you do, I promise that you will write faster and with greater effectiveness.

Further Essay-Writing Tips: Word Counts

Working with word counts has become the norm for the modern writer, and those pursuing essay-based subjects will inevitably develop an all too intimate relationship with the word count figure at the bottom of the screen. Make sure you use this aspect of modern writing to your advantage by following these tips.

Always work to the word count provided. Most assigned academic essays come with a word limit; you must pay close attention to this word limit and never go too far above or below it. Seek out the rules surrounding your essay and the word count. At some institutions you will lose marks if you go over or under the word limit by a certain amount. On these occasions in particular, be sure to strictly follow the word limit.

Even if there is no set penalty for going above or below the word limit, always respect the limit and attempt to stay as close to it as you can. Handing in an essay that doesn't respect the limit will frustrate whoever is marking it. It will appear, at the very least, that you are not aware of the form requirements, and at worst will mean you lose marks as a penalty.

Throughout the essay, it can be helpful to set yourself word count targets. Perhaps attempt to write 500 or 1,000 words per hour. This will keep you moving forward and push you to write through any blocks you might experience. However, do not become obsessive with the word count, as habitually checking it will distract you from writing quality content at a good speed.

It is inevitable that you will, at some point, find yourself obsessively looking at the word count, with a sense of frustration as it grows all too slowly: 10, 20, 50 words at a time. This is a sign of a kind of "writer's block" and can be caused by one or a combination of the following.

...you haven't done enough research and simply don't have a sufficient amount to say because you don't know enough. To remedy this, simply give yourself perhaps another couple of hours to find quality material, ensuring it correlates directly to the essay and gives you clear points and evidence to include.

...you haven't planned effectively, and the order or content of the essay is generally unclear, or at the very least, you haven't established what the next step is. Return to your plan and continue revising it, extending it, and making it clearer. It may be that all you need to do is find the next step, so again return to your plan and identify the logical next step. Perhaps you will have to leave altogether the topic you were trying to work on in order to move to a topic you can write on more easily.

...you aren't moving the essay in the right direction. If it seems difficult to make any headway, perhaps you are attempting to write on topics/subtopics that just don't contain enough material for you to write on. Additionally, you might be arguing for something incoherent or illogical. If this is the case, go back to basics. Return to the title and make sure it is clear and that you understand it. Perhaps make a basic mind map to help reveal the clearest steps you can take to overcome the impasse. Further research also might be helpful here.

Further Essay Writing Tips: Discover and Imitate Good Writing Styles

If you will be writing many essays during your academic career or perhaps want to enter a profession that requires a lot of writing, it is a great idea to familiarize yourself with and begin to imitate better writing styles.

All writers develop a certain style with their writing. To develop your own in a positive way, read many texts that are similar to the style you wish to emulate. Don't feel ashamed to imitate. There are many different ways to present an idea, and it is important to be aware of them. If you incorporate different styles to your own writing, you will be creating something new. It will be writing with your "twist". You cannot imitate a style completely.

If you are only going to be writing academic pieces, always think about presenting things in a clear fashion. Therefore, you should incorporate the styles of writers who do this. Some of the textbooks required for your course may be written in a powerful and clear manner, while others may not be. Asking your teacher or lecturer which they find well written is a great way to reveal which you should be focusing on.

BONUS SECTION: HOW TO STUDY

Introduction

The aim of this book is to give you tips to make your time studying as successful and enjoyable as possible. It contains my best advice on time management, goal setting, and how to get the best grades with the least effort. It's advice that also transfers brilliantly well to professionals, the self-employed, and anyone who manages their own projects and/or daily work cycle.

(If you fall into the non-student category, whenever you see the word "study" throughout this book, think the word "work" instead, and whenever you see "grades" think "work goals".)

There's nothing more to say, so let's get started!

Build the Study Habit and Schedule Study Times

One of the main reasons students don't get good grades is simple: they don't have the study habit. Being able to regularly make yourself sit down and learn the necessary material is an essential part of becoming a great student.

Both when you study and the length of time you study for should be as regular and routine as possible. This will make the habit of studying easier to begin and sustain over time. Working at the same time every day is the best way to do this, e.g., between 7 and 9 every morning. (This time works well as it is before classes.) Of course, your study time will depend on the courses you are taking and your other commitments.

Working at set times every day will help build the habit of studying. There will be less urge to procrastinate and do unimportant tasks because you know when you should be working and when you shouldn't. Eventually it will actually take more willpower not to study at these times because you will subconsciously expect to be utilizing your study time.

Time Box Tasks

To build a sense of urgency and avoid being overwhelmed with work, it is helpful to create definite periods of time or 'time boxes' in which you work.

Set a timer and do not work for more or less than the time you set. Then, take a break for a small timed period. Rinse and repeat. Working like this will help you overcome procrastination because you will not feel the sense of being overwhelmed by a project. One of the main reasons that students (or anyone) procrastinate is that they feel anxious about not knowing how to begin and/or that they will have to keep working for a long time. By limiting the time spent working on something to a set number, we can alleviate anxiety caused by either of these problems.

Working for a definite amount of time also helps stop perfectionism and curbs the desire to spend more time on a project than is necessary. Many people suffer from this. They work long hours to make their project as perfect as it can possibly be. Sometimes this leads to people doing great things. However, it is more often an enemy of productivity as it leads to a task dragging on for longer than needed. For example, if it takes 10 hours to complete an assignment to a 70 percent standard, is it worth working 20 hours to complete it to a 72 percent standard? Sometimes yes, but usually no. Time boxing is an excellent tool for stopping perfectionism in its tracks. It forces us to complete a task to a good standard and no more.

Both for study sessions and for whole projects, many students find they work more effectively by working to a time scale. In doing so, you will create a greater sense of urgency to your work, as you only think about continuing work until the timer sounds. The alternative of working for an unspecified amount of time makes both beginning and continuing work more difficult. It also encourages a slow, non-urgent work mode and/or perfectionism. To avoid this, use time boxing and set time limits for your work.

Prioritize Assignments and Be Aware of Grade Boundaries/Percentages

The extent to which a project affects your grade and how long it takes to complete will vary in relation to one another. Therefore, it is important to spend more time on those projects that contribute more marks and less on those that don't.

At the beginning of the academic year, you should deconstruct your course so that you know what percentage each module/exam/project will contribute toward the final grade. This will reveal which areas require more time and effort than others. It will often not be clear what the more valuable modules are until you do this.

You can then place more emphasis on the areas that contribute more to your overall grade and limit time spent on the less valuable. Re-adjust where you are placing your time and effort as you receive feedback throughout the year. Be flexible and note where you are struggling to get the grades you want. When you receive marks for coursework, rework these into your plans. For example, if you do very well in a piece of coursework, scale back the time you planned to spend revising for its corresponding exam, and instead, prepare for an exam on a topic you are struggling with. There is no way to perfectly balance this, as it will be based on guesswork. Simply do your best, and work as intelligently as you can.

Test Yourself Frequently

Always being aware of exactly how well you are progressing toward your final grade is essential in order to adjust your study plans and better understand what you need to work on. Apart from coursework and feedback in class, testing yourself is the best way to do this.

Gather past exam papers/questions and frequently test yourself with them. Ideally, use entire test papers from previous years (assuming the course hasn't changed too drastically). Also, test yourself in conditions similar to how you will take the actual exam. Giving yourself the same amount of time as you will get in the real exam is crucial. Set a timer and stick to it. Once you have completed the exam paper, mark it yourself or give it to a teacher/lecturer/fellow student to mark. Make sure whoever is marking it does so by following a correct answer sheet/mark scheme.

Ascertaining what level you are currently working at will reveal where your subsequent studies should concentrate. For example if you are working on an essay-based exam, you might learn that the content of your writing is fine, but the quantity needs to increase. In this case, you can take further practice tests and simply work to write faster.

Start Work Early

Many people find studying in the morning works best for them. Try this yourself and see if you can join the club. Getting your studies out of the way first thing is an excellent way to get more studying done.

Starting work early is often easier because there is less chance of getting distracted and becoming involved doing other things. Watching TV, Internet browsing, or relaxing with friends are often best left until after you have done your studying. These activities then become rewards instead of distractions, and you can enjoy the rest of the day without worry that you should have done more. Studying earlier in the day within a definite "time box," before you have a chance to get distracted by anything else, is a great way to increase the efficiency of your studying and enjoy your days more.

Have Fun Away From Your Studies

If you work intelligently, there is no need to work non-stop. Plan many breaks, and arrange for fun! Enjoyable activities boost your focus and memory. In the same way that muscles need rest after exercise to grow, so too your mind needs to relax after it is exerted.

It is helpful to get as far away as possible from your study and work habits. Take time to travel to another city, another country, or simply try to do something new. Getting away and having fun will mean that when you do return to studying, you will be completely ready to learn, to work hard, and get the best grades you are capable of.

Create Study Routines: 60-60-30, 50-50-10

Creating definite study routines will allow you to better manage your time. It is difficult and unsustainable to work constantly for hours at a time, so implement regular patterns in which you alternate between working and taking breaks. This is short-scale time boxing applied to a rigorous work/rest pattern.

Experiment with what works best for you as different stretches of concentration work well for different people. Some prefer a longer four hour work session to get into "flow," while others prefer shorter ones so as to never feel overwhelmed by a project.

An example work/rest study routine that fits well into a normal day is to work for a 50 minute period followed by a 10 minute break, and every four hours take an hour break for a meal.

However, there are no hard and fast rules. You might prefer to work for 90 minutes at a time, and then take a 30 minute break. The aim is to find what works well for you so that you can sustain working for a long period of time with good focus and minimum fatigue.

If you feel exhausted or too mentally strained with a routine, then work for smaller cycles. You can always increase the work time lengths if it seems doable later.

Make sure to always use a timer, and stop working when it sounds, even if you want to continue. You often won't be aware that you need a break when you actually do. If you become successful with this habit, you will find you can create work-rest routines that are generative and allow you to work with focus for 6, 8, 10, or even 12 hour days whilst still feeling good.

Minimize Possible Distractions and Eliminate Multi-Tasking

One of the greatest enemies to successful work in the modern age is the abundance of distractions. When you are studying, it is imperative to make sure that you study and do nothing else. Your ability to focus all of your attention on the task at hand is a powerful asset. Attempting to do more than one thing at a time or switching between activities jeopardizes this.

Turn off your mobile phone and close the internet browser. If these remain a possible distraction, make it as difficult as possible to access them. For example, turn off your phone and put it out of sight or out of reach. Consider giving it to a friend or leaving it in another room until you are finished working.

These distractions will compromise how effectively you work, and even worse, can lead to you stopping work altogether. Just checking a website or your phone for a moment can cause a series of internal triggers, and in no time you will lose the motivation and focus you had. This can be a big obstacle for students and employees alike. If this sounds like your past studying attempts, make eliminating distractions a priority.

Set Goals for Grades

Setting goals for the grades you want will make it easier to ascertain the level of work required to receive them. The goal of simply "getting the best grades you can" is good, but not good enough. These goals need to be more specific and ideally very specific. Many students already have goals for the grades they want to achieve. If you don't have any, start thinking about what yours could be now.

Having clear goals for the grades you want will make it easier to ascertain what you need to learn in order to achieve them. This is partly achieved by saving you from wasting time learning things you don't need to. Some skills and information might take a lot of time to learn, but if they are beyond what you need to learn it will be a waste of time. For example, for an essay-based exam, there is no use learning a large amount of quotations (enough to get an A) if your target is a B grade and your grasp of concepts isn't nearly strong enough to get a B.

Goals for grades will also allow you to celebrate successes and push you to do more when needed.

Once you have decided what your target grades are, find out precisely what you need to work on in order to achieve them. Then build your study schedule around working on these areas (with regular testing to ensure you are progressing well).

Clarify Study Session Goals

Every time you sit down to study, you should be clear about what you are going to do and what you want to gain from the session. Planning to "study for module A" won't be nearly as effective as "50 minutes reading and annotating chapter 1." It is far too easy to study aimlessly while naively believing that you are learning. Working in this fuzzy, diffused way will often mean you don't learn or progress in your work. Instead, have focused, clear targets each time you sit.

At the end of the study session, you will also be able to check off the task, and this will also help you feel more motivated to continue on. The sense of incremental progress with each completed study session will build momentum and make each successive study session easier.

Detach from Work While on Breaks

When you take a short break from work, it is very important that you really do take a break.

If you are studying at a computer screen (perhaps you are writing up some lecture notes), the break you take must be away from the computer. If you are taking only 10 minute breaks every hour, it is important to make this break a time for your mind and body to separate from what you have been working on.

If you are working at a computer, opening a new browser and checking a news channel or a social networking site is no longer working, but is it truly taking a break? Not really. Instead, move away from the desk and away from the computer. Do something physical. Maybe take a walk or lie down. At the very least, don't look at a screen. The break needs to be spent on something different from what you have been doing. If you have been sitting at a computer screen, lying down outside on the grass for 10 minutes could help you to unwind sufficiently.

You might find it helpful to engage your mind with something else altogether. If you don't engage your mind with something else, like a video game or book, you might find your mind racing on with what you were doing. To get more mental separation and a better break, consider doing something that takes your attention away from what you were working on altogether.

Why are you at School/College/University?

Knowing exactly what you want from your course and what you are going to do afterward will further help you to focus and study well.

Perhaps you are career-driven and want to go into a certain industry after your course. If this is the case, research the job role you want, how much money you want to be earning, where you want to work, etc. Getting details will help you feel grounded and motivated to continue on with the course.

For some students, there is no definite job role at the end. This does not mean that you cannot find a clear purpose for studying hard. Maybe you enjoy the subject and want to study it for this reason alone. If this is the case, consider concrete things you can do to get more from it. This could be getting an article in your field published.

Understanding why you are studying and what you really want from your course is a great way to further boost your focus and enjoyment.

Find a Study Partner and/or a Study Group

Studying with other people is a great way to get more from your course.

Depending on your preferences for working and your personality, this can be a fantastic prospect or a daunting one. However, creating a study group, or at the very least one person with whom you regularly work, can help a lot. Explaining topics and quizzing one another will boost your comprehension and ensure that you thoroughly understand the material.

Make sure you choose the right people to study with. It might not be best to study with a friend you also go out partying with. Additionally, make sure you study with people of a similar ability. 'Carrying' someone who is struggling won't be productive.

Working in a group can be a brilliant idea as well. This can be the most enjoyable way to work, especially if you are naturally highly social. Working in a group helps you to motivate one another and can provide many points of view.

Perfect Necessary Skills and Seek Feedback

There will inevitably be skills within your subject you need to master. These skills will usually require someone else to critique your ability. Seek as much feedback as possible in order to improve these skills.

Whether you are working in a laboratory or writing essays, the skills you have to develop cannot be marked and improved on entirely by yourself. You need an expert. This person will often be a teacher assigned to you. It might then be a matter of luck how helpful their critiques are and whether they are offered as regularly as you require them. If they aren't offered enough or aren't helpful enough, seek another tutor from the establishment to replace and/or work alongside to provide extra help.

In cases such as essay writing, you will need to practice regularly. Practice even if your work won't be marked. The more feedback you can get the better, so it doesn't hurt to ask other teachers to critique your work as well.

Whatever the skill set you are trying to develop, practice properly, practice regularly, seek feedback and then improve. Use this process again and again, until you develop your skill set into an art form.

Build a Relationship with a Tutor/Mentor

Having a go-between for you and your school/establishment will prove very helpful. Many centers will provide you with a 'tutor,' i.e., someone you meet with regularly in order to discuss your progress. If yours doesn't provide this extra help, find someone who can take on this role for you.

Your tutor can provide guidance for your course and let you know what to expect. He or she can answer questions on any number of things. For example, a tutor might help you to find old exam papers to work from, or find out where an exam will be seated.

If anything goes wrong during your course and you need help (perhaps you fall ill and need an extension on a project), help and advice from your tutor could be essential. Also, if you have moved away from home and need guidance on everyday issues, for example, money management, eating out, etc. Having someone older who can guide you will make life easier.

Thank you

Thank you for making it to the end of both books. If you enjoyed them, please leave a review on the Amazon website.

All the best,

John Connelly

WITHDRAWN
★ FROM ★
STOCK

Printed in Great Britain
by Amazon